Working
Can Make You
grumpy

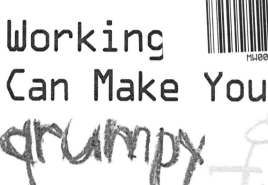

ii

Working Too Much Can Make You grumpy

kids talk about why it's
good to not work too much.

edited by

Debra A. Dinnocenzo

Mancini
McClintock
Press

Published by Mancini-M'Clintock Press

Printed in the United States of America
10 9 8 7 6 5 4 3 2 1

Excerpts with permission from **Dot Calm: The Search for Sanity in a Wired World**
by Debra A. Dinnocenzo & Richard B. Swegan   (Berrett-Koehler Publishers © 2001)

Cover design by Sabol Design (Cover graphic contributed by Madison Spanfelner)

Library of Congress Control Number: 2006909894

ISBN # 0-9742902-0-3

For permission requests, inquiries, or to order additional copies of this publication, contact:

Virtual Works!

10592 Perry Hwy., Suite 201
Wexford, PA 15090   USA

Tel: 724.934.9349
Fax: 724.934.9348

info@virtualworkswell.com

www.virtualworkswell.com

Dedication

**For my daughter,
Jennimarie,
who always gives me a good reason
to not work too much.**

vi

Acknowledgments

Without the children who completed the survey, this book could not have been written. For these children...as well as their insights and touchingly honest telling of the truth...I express my deepest gratitude. I offer special thanks to Anna Arnn for her eloquent and profound response, from which the title emerged.

I also appreciate the participation of various institutions and programs for children. Without the support of the leaders of these organizations, my access to the real authors would have been limited.

I'm very thankful for the contributions of my graduate students during the last several years. These students assisted my research efforts (and helped their grades!) by interviewing kids about why it's good to not work too much.

Finally, I thank you—for buying this book, for reading it, and for sharing it with others. It's by far one of shortest books you'll ever read...from which you'll receive the longest benefit if you remember each day its simple and provocative message.

Children enter the world radiating
the Spirit—
learn from them of innocence
and simplicity

Psalms for Praying
by Nan Merrill

X

Preface

When I published ***Dot Calm: The Search for Sanity in a Wired World*** with my husband and co-author, Rick Swegan, our daughter (then 7 years old) graciously contributed the Special Foreword aptly titled, "Why it's Good to Not Work Too Much." In the course of our research for that book, hundreds of adults shared with us their feelings about problems associated with overwork. The continual struggle for right-sized work lives and a reasonable balance between work and personal commitments is a constant challenge for nearly everyone who participated in our research.

In spite of the wealth of information concerning overwork difficulties and solutions garnered from our research participants, I remained intrigued by the observations of children regarding these issues. And since we all know how strikingly honest and poignant children can be through their innocent reporting of the truth, I continued to ponder what we might learn from them.

While co-teaching a graduate course on "Leadership in the Virtual Workplace," Rick and I covered the topics of overwork, over-access, and over-connectedness in the digital age. During this section we asked our students, all of whom were experienced workers actively employed across a variety of occupations and industries, to undertake a little research project. Their assignment one week was to find three people under the age of 10 and to ask them why it's good to not work too much. The responses exceeded our expectations, in terms of quantity and content. Further, the reactions of our work-weary students (inherently overworked as a result of pursuing a graduate degree while fully employed), were themselves stunning. One student submitted the following in response to the assignment:

> *My 3 year-old son: "I know daddy works hard so he can get things for me, but I don't want you to go to work."* *(Broke my heart completely in half.) My 6-1/2 year old daughter: "I don't like when you're not here to read to me and color with me, I miss you, why do you have to go to work?" (She broke the two halves of previously broken heart.)*

We ourselves were heartbroken to read the response of another child who offered a reason why parents working too much is not so good:

> "I can't have a little sister."

One of our graduate students reported that "this was the hardest assignment of the class." Another had a flash of insight from an experience he reported as part of this assignment:

> *A few years ago, I was a very busy person. You know, striving for the American dream of success and money, etc. I was home one late afternoon and my wife and I and our son were sitting on our porch. My son said, "Can I go down to Billy's house?" I piped up and said, "Yes." He then looked at my wife and said, "Can I, Mom?" Wow! In our mutually respectful household, I suddenly realized that I wasn't home enough. I am now.*

I came to understand even more clearly that an eternal truth abounded here—if only we ask our children, they'll tell us!   And so I did. I asked a wide range of kids about what work their parents do, why work is a good thing, and – most importantly – what the problems are with working too much.

Of course I realize that most parents work out of necessity. And the good news is that most kids understand that. Naturally, they see the reasons for work through their kid-centric view of the world. So while you might work to pay the mortgage or rent, buy food, invest for the future, etc., your kids generally believe that you work primarily to buy stuff for them! And, ultimately, that's probably true, but kids reduce this to the most fundamental necessities according to their view of the world.

As for the problems with working too much, kids offer no shortage of observations and implications on this issue. And I offer them now to you. Feast on this amazing food for thought...and think deeply about how you live your life, the choices you make, the tradeoffs you make, and if you are investing your time and energy wisely.

Better yet—ask your kids. They will tell you the stark truth and, perhaps, offer you a gentle and compelling wake-up call. Moving beyond the admonishment to "wake up and smell the coffee" or "wake up and smell the roses," I encourage you to "wake up and ask the kids." They'll tell it like it is—or like it should be.

Debra A. Dinnocenzo
Wexford, Pennsylvania, USA
2006

Why working too much is not good...

2

You can't
go on
vacation.

You can get fat because you don't have time to go to the gym.

My parents are always in a bad mood and yell at me more when they work too much.

Never get
to read
to your kids.

If you work too much you will get tired and sick.

I feel
like I am
not
important.

People need to play too. They can go to the movies or play a game. Or fix things.

You don't spend enough time with God.

You can
be with your
family more
by not
working so
much.

You get
exhausted,
and being
exhausted
stinks.

I do not
get any
attention.

Mommy
is
cranky.

If you work too
much you get
stressed and
are always busy.

So your bones
don't hurt
when you
have to get up
early in the
morning.

You will get
too tired
to play if you
work too much.

Working too much would make my Daddy's computer explode and would make his brain come out of his head.

My parents often
don't hear what
I say to them
or they don't listen
closely enough and
I have to say it
again.

You can't spend time with your friends and family and have time to focus on things that are more fun like making your children happy.

My parents make us go to bed early so they can have some peace and quiet.

When my daddy works so much, I never get to read my favorite stories.

You can
get a
headache.

You
do not
get any
fun.

It's not safe
to work
too much.

My parents can't come to my games after school.

Work is boring and play is fun.

If people work away from home, they may not spend enough time with their family. And if they work with a computer screen, they may damage their eyes. If you are a firefighter, you might get stuck with your job and may not be able to come home to see your family.

If you work
too much
your head
will explode.

You can't sleep in.

When people
work too much,
they might get
sick.

You think
about work
even when
you're not
working.

You smile more when you're not working.

People who
work too much
get tired and
mean.

I cannot see
my Daddy more.

When my parents are really tired after work, they become forgetful.

You can't
get your
nails done.

So they won't
be grumpy,
mean
or
tired.

Working too much will make you upset and you might be bossy. And no one will be happy with the bossy person.

If you work
too much,
you can
get sick of
your job.

You can get
frustrated
and have
stress.

If you work
too much,
you can
hurt
your brain.

Working
too much
leaves you
hungry
all the time.

Working too
much makes you
too tired
and also makes
it harder for you
to concentrate.

Dad's way too tired, cranky and doesn't want to listen to me.

My parents
don't play with
me when they
work too much.

Never
get to do
anything
you want.

You will be
unhappy
and
moody.

People
can forget
to be
kind
to their
family.

They would have a
heart attack,
then they would
have to stop
working and their
job wouldn't get
done at all.

You
can't
go shopping.

If you work too much, your brain will get mixed up. You will be putting down the right answer for the wrong subject.

You have no time for your children and may have health problems.

You can't
drink beer
in the
hot tub.

You shouldn't work too much because it distracts you from more important things (like daughters).

You can't go to the store to buy food (but then you can go to McDonalds!).

You
could get
a
migraine.

Daddy could
eat dinner
with us.

Everyone needs a rest so that they're relaxed and happy.

When
people are not
working,
they do
parties.

If they work
too much, they
might not have
fun—
and everyone
needs to have
fun.

You
might have
too much
money.

You could take us to the park or watch a movie with us by the fireplace.

Working too much takes time away from other things that need to be done.

You
won't want
to work
anymore.

You get
worn out
and
can't play.

You can't
go see
a friend.

My parents don't want to be bothered with me when they work too much.

It would be better and easier not to work so hard.

70

Let us remember
to live our lives abundantly…
take time for
your priorities that,
in the end,
really matter…
take care of yourself
and those you love,
for you may not be with them
tomorrow…
and choose wisely,
for your choices define
both the limits and
possibilities
of your life.

Excerpted from:

Dot Calm: The Search for Sanity in a Wired World

71

Little Baby Stary

Once upon a time, there was a female star and a male star. They were married and had a child called Stary Jr. They were happy with what they had. The End

Jennimarie

Jennimarie Dinnocenzo Swegan, age 5 (1998)

73

74

75